BADGES OF THE BRITISH ARMY
1820 to 1987
An illustrated reference guide
for collectors

BADGES OF THE BRITISH ARMY

1820 to 1987

An illustrated reference guide for collectors

F. Wilkinson

The Naval & Military Press Ltd

Published by

The Naval & Military Press Ltd
Unit 10 Ridgewood Industrial Park,
Uckfield, East Sussex,
TN22 5QE England

Tel: +44 (0) 1825 749494
Fax: +44 (0) 1825 765701

www.naval-military-press.com
www.military-genealogy.com
www.militarymaproom.com

CONTENTS

PREFACE

This book first appeared in 1969 and has since run to six editions. The author and publishers feel that it is now time to produce a new version incorporating knowledge and experience gained during the intervening period.

The book differs from previous editions in that it attempts to extend its coverage by including a few badges that, perhaps, do not fall strictly within the original scope. This has been done to indicate some less obvious fields of badge collecting, for it is a sad fact that the popularity of badges has led to an increase in prices and this restricts the opportunities of many collectors. Another very unfortunate result of this great interest has been the increased production of fakes, copies and restrikes. In the early days these copies were reasonably easy to spot, but sadly the skill of the producers has increased to such a degree that it is often difficult to be sure that any item is genuine and original. All the badges illustrated are originals, the majority having been collected long before restrikes appeared in quantity.

The layout of the book has also been changed, the items being arranged differently in the hope that it will prove easier for the reader to identify and value badges. In a book of this size it is impossible to do more than show a selection of the tremendous variety of badges, and a bibliography has been included for those who wish to extend their interest.

The dates included in the captions show the period for which the badges were generally in use, but it must be stressed that in many cases regiments did not always comply with new regulations and continued to wear badges that were officially out of date.

Once again the author is indebted to Jim Burgess who cheerfully disorganized his home, and his collection in order that it could be photographed. His trust and kindness are greatly appreciated.

The photographs were taken by Paul Forrester who has long suffered the author's photographic demands. On this occasion faulty film and other problems added to his heavy burden. As always, he overcame all difficulties with good humour and professional competence.

Finally the author must thank Laurie Archer who, over the years, has proved a staunch friend, answering queries and providing authoritative information on a range of obscure badges and other topics with superb expertise and good humour.

F. Wilkinson, London, 1987

INTRODUCTION

The standardization of badges in the British Army dates from the eighteenth century. Prior to this, regiments were usually known by the name of their colonel or commanding officer. Badges varied, but often incorporated the coat-of-arms of the colonel. A change of commanding officer meant a change of title and probably a change of badge.

In 1751 an order was issued which saw the introduction of a more standard system of identifying units. Infantry regiments were numbered and some were allowed to incorporate authorized special designs as part of their badges. By this date, symbols such as the dragon, the white horse of Hanover and the Prince of Wales's Feathers were already in use and were to remain with various regiments right up to the present. Mottoes were also incorporated in badges and at this early date the most common was *Nec Espera Terrent* (Nor do Difficulties Deter).

These badges and mottoes were mostly worn on the various styles of head-dress, usually embroidered on the cloth caps, but they also appeared on another piece of equipment – the shoulder belt plate (see 1–14). This item of uniform developed during the later part of the 18th century when the belt was moved from the waist to cross the chest and shoulders. At first the plates were usually small, oval and fairly simple, but later ones were rectangular and much more elaborate. Those for the other ranks were normally of stamped brass and most were impressed or engraved with the regimental number. Later, name, crest, motto and often battle honours were included. Those for the officers were much more elaborate and were made up of several components held together by pierced lugs and thin wire.

Various styles of head-dress had been worn by the infantry at different periods, but in 1800 the famous shako, known from its cylindrical shape as the stovepipe, was adopted. At the front

9

was fitted a large rectangular metal badge, and as usual there was a difference in quality between those worn by officers and those worn by other ranks. The basic plate had the crowned royal cypher GR, together with military trophies, but regiments with special emblems were allowed to include them on the plate. In 1812 the style of shako was changed and the plate became smaller and was shaped like a shield, but like its predecessor, displayed the royal cipher and often had some regimental distinctions (see 4).

This style of head-dress underwent various modifications as changing fashion led to its becoming bell-topped, and then cylindrical again with the advent of the Albert shako in 1844. The style of badge was also changed, becoming star-shaped and much more elaborate.

In 1855 the shoulder belt plate was abolished except for Scottish units, and in the same year a low crowned shako was adopted. This, in a variety of forms, lasted until 1878 when the Home Service Pattern Helmet was introduced. This cloth and cork helmet had a large, elaborate, star-shaped badge and a top central spike or, for the corps, a ball-and-cup fitting. Like previous styles of badge, those for other ranks were usually of stamped brass while those for officers were made up of several components (see 16).

In 1874 a new style of undress cap, the glengarry, was adopted and this had its own badge which usually had the regimental number within a circlet. Until 1881 almost all army badges had carried the regimental number, but in that year far-sweeping reforms of the army were introduced by Lord Cardwell. Numbers were discarded and names substituted, and in 1885 the glengarry was abandoned.

Cavalry head-dress has nearly always been much more elaborate than that of the infantry and in consequence the badges were usually larger and more decorative. The lancers, introduced in the early 19th century, wore a distinctive *tschapka* cap which was based on the head-dress of the Polish lancers and had a large crescent-shaped plate. The Lifeguards and other mounted units wore metal helmets, often surmounted by plumes and with large central front plates. Today's armoured and mobile units, which are the descendants of the cavalry, regiments, wear badges that are little different from those of the infantry.

Distinction must be made between the various sections of the armed forces. In addition to the standing regular army there were the militia, the volunteers, the yeomanry and later the Territorial Army. Each group wore badges similar to those of the regulars, but often differing in details; consequently, identification can be difficult. One guiding feature is that the basic colour of badges for regular army units was 'gold', while for milita it was 'silver'. This rule of thumb must be used cautiously: most Scottish units also favour 'silver' badges.

The vast majority of badges offered to the collector will date from the mid to late nineteenth century onwards, and dating them can be a problem, but there are some general rules which can often help. It should be stressed, however, that these rules are only guides and there are exceptions to all of them. The crown is the first indication of date. Badges of Queen Victoria's reign (1837–1901) will have a queen's crown with its dome-shaped appearance (see **19**). Badges of King Edward VIII (1901–10), George V (1910–36) and George VI (1936–52) had the crown changed (see **16**) and this type is known as the king's crown. The accession of Queen Elizabeth II in 1952 saw the adoption of another style of crown and to distinguish between the two queens that of Victoria is usually abbreviated to QVC.

If the badge incorporates a regimental number it probably pre-dates 1881 when the reforms abandoning numbers were introduced. Regimental titles have changed over the years and these, too, can help date a piece. Obviously the style of badge is a vital dating feature, and reference to the examples illustrated may give some guidance in the identifying of similar pieces. Mottoes can also be helpful although some are used by more than one regiment.

The most commonly used materials in badge manufacture were gilding metal, usually described as brass by many collectors (as it is in this book), and white metal. Those badges composed of both are described as bimetal), while many officers' badges were of bronze. In times of shortage, as happened during the World Wars, some badges were produced in an economy style; those which had usually been of bimetal were made in brass. During the Second World War brass was often replaced by plastic. In 1952 a new material, usually referred to as Staybrite, was introduced. This anodized aluminium gave the badges a rather gaudy, cheap appearance and they are generally unpopular, but they are a cheap starting-point for a collector of limited means!

While metal badges are the most sought after, there are many interesting cloth badges, although they are often in poor condition, the material being more susceptible to damage. Again, one or two examples have been included.

Restrikes struck from original dies or copied from originals using modern hi-tech methods have become a major hazard for the badge collector and today their quality is extremely high. Detection can be very difficult and is largely a matter of experience. This statement is easy to make, but for the collector experience is a difficult thing to acquire. One of the best ways is to haunt the dealers, markets, auction houses, collecting societies and museums, taking every opportunity to look at and, above all, to handle badges. Look at the degree and position of wear, look at the back and observe how the lugs or sliders are fitted and observe the quality of the detail. Whenever possible compare the restrike with known originals or with photographs of the genuine piece and it may be possible to pinpoint minor differences. If the collector is happy to have a copy of a rare badge, there can be no objection to restrikes, but if the aim is to acquire original badges, restrikes are not appropriate. There is also the problem of the unscrupulous or unknowing dealer who tries to sell a restrike as an original. In the end the old adage *Caveat emptor* (Let the buyer beware) is probably the best advice. If a collector finds a good reliable dealer ready to offer guarantees, he has found a 'treasure'.

The majority of badges illustrated are from British Army head-dress, but there were other types including proficiency badges, collar badges (commonly known as dogs), shoulder titles and divisional signs. All have their collectors and a few examples have been included. Fortunately there are now a number of authoritative books dealing with these themes and the collector will find them listed in the bibliography.

Badge collecting lends itself to many approaches and the collector may well find that his original concept becomes modified as knowledge and the collection grow. It is probably true to say that most collectors begin with the object of putting together a large collection of badges with little idea of making any selection. This somewhat 'jackdaw' approach often changes as a particular interest begins to develop, and some collectors begin to specialize. The number of options is very large. Some concentrate on one particular regiment and seek to acquire as many of its badges as possible. The group on Plate **6** is an example of the variety of badges used by one unit, yet that particular collection is far from complete. Another approach is to concentrate on a particular campaign and seek out badges of those regiments that served in it. Theme collections can be made with the aim of acquiring badges with a common feature such as animals, coats-of-arms, plants or castles. Yet another approach might be to specialize in a period and collect units that were serving in the 1950s, for example.

Once a theme or period has been selected the obvious question is, where does the collector look for the material? The days when most markets or antique shops had a 'junk' box, which often held a few badges at prices well within a youthful enthusiast's pocket, have long since gone. The very popularity of badge collecting has forced prices up and the hobby is now quite big business and this in turn has attracted some dealers who are, perhaps, not quite as careful as they might be, and who do not always describe their wares as accurately as they should.

One of the greatest hazards for the modern collector is the restrike. As suggested, if a collector is satisfied to have a modern copy in his collection there is no problem. The infuriating thing is to find that the 'rare' badge, which cost a fair amount and seemed so genuine, is only a restrike. It would be less than honest to suggest that it is easy to spot these impostors; many a well-established collector has been misled. It must be said yet again that the only defences are experience and a reliable supplier.

Some dealers offer a guarantee and they should be supported. There is also an implied guarantee by the auction houses most of whom will refund the purchase price if a badge can be shown to be not as catalogued. Apart from the auction houses and specialist dealers, the other sources are the obvious ones of fellow collectors, antique-shops and markets. There are several societies devoted to badge collecting and associated topics, and a subscription to these is well worthwhile for the contacts, advice and information contained in their newsletters or magazines. Jumble sales, boot sales and the street markets are also worth some attention although it must be said that these are no longer the happy hunting-grounds they once were.

13

Perseverance is an essential characteristic of the badge collector, but the pleasure of finding a desirable badge will be reward enough and may help to compensate for all the fruitless searches. Displaying the collection is very much a personal choice, but whichever method is used the prime consideration must be the preservation of the badge. The old methods of nailing them to boards, drilling holes in the slider, bending and twisting lugs and even breaking them off must be avoided at all costs. One simple method is to mount them on card or polystyrene tiles which can be covered with material or painted, and cut to accommodate the sliders and lugs. Mounted in glazed frames, they make attractive wall decorations. Shallow drawers are convenient, but the badges are obviously less easily viewed. Before any display is mounted it is most important to plan the lay-out, remembering to leave gaps for any badges that may be needed to complete a sequence.

Most collectors like to clean their badges and there are many proprietary polishes on the market, the least abrasive should always be used to reduce wear on the badge. Some collectors like to lacquer their cleaned badges, but many deplore the idea. It should be pointed out that many lacquers discolour and crack and some can be very difficult to remove. On balance it is probably better not to lacquer, but obviously each collector must reach his own conclusion.

However the badges are displayed, it is important to compile a comprehensive catalogue, preferably with photographs. Not only is it useful for reference, but it will also be invaluable for insurance; it can be a shock to discover how the value of a collection has grown. It is worth considering the use of one of the invisible security inks to mark the badges so that positive identification is assured in the event of recovery from loss or theft.

Badge collecting is still one of the cheaper hobbies and can stimulate all manner of interests and encourage research into so many fields such as weapons, uniforms, medals, regimental histories, biographies, campaigns, war games and social history. Above all it is a hobby that will offer its supporters many hours of pleasure, the chance to meet fellow enthusiasts and even, on rare occasions, some financial benefit.

BIBLIOGRAPHY

Anon. *Badges and Emblems of the British Forces 1940.* London, 1968

Almack, E. *Regimental Badges worn in the British Army 100 years ago.* London, 1970

Bloomer, W., and Bloomer, K. *Badges of the Highland and Lowland Regiments.* London, 1982

— *Scottish Regimental Badges 1793–1971.* London, 1982

Carman, W. Y. *Glengarry Badges of the British Line Regiments to 1881.* London, 1973

Chichester, H., and Burgess-Short, G. *Records and Badges of Every Regiment and Corps in the British Army.* (repr.) London, 1986

Churchill, C., and Westlake, R. *British Army Collar Badges 1881 to the Present.* London, 1986

Cole, H. N. *Badges on Battledress.* London, 1953

Cox, R. H. W. *Military Badges of the British Empire.* London, 1982

Edwards, T. J. *Regimental Badges.* London, 1968

Gaylor, J. *Military Badge Collecting.* London, 1977

Kipling, A. L., and King, H. L. *Head-Dress Badges of the British Army.* vol 1, London, 1978; vol 2, London, 1979

May, W., Carman, W. and Tanner, J. *Badges and Insignia of the British Armed Services.* London, 1974

Mollo, A., and McGregor, M. *Naval, Marine and Air Force Uniforms of World War 2.* London, 1975

Norman, C. B. *Battle Honours of the British Army.* London, 1911

Parkyn, H. G. *Shoulder Belt Plates and Buttons.* Aldershot, 1956

Rawlings, K. *British Military Badges.* Bournemouth, 1977

Ripley, H. *Buttons of the British Army 1855–1970.* London, 1971

Rosignoli, G. *Army Badges and Insignia of World War 2.* vol 1, London, 1972; vol 2, London, 1975

— *Army Badges and Insignia since 1945.* London, 1973

— *Air Force Badges and Insignia of World War 2.* London, 1976

Westlake, R. *A Register of Territorial Force Cadet Units 1910–22.* Wembley, 1984

— *The Rifle Volunteers.* Chippenham, 1982

— *The Territorial Battalions.* Tunbridge Wells, 1986

White, A. S. *A Bibliography of the Regimental Histories of the British Army.* London, 1965

Periodicals which have occasional articles about badges

Journal of Military Historical Society

Journal of the Society for Army Historical Research

Military Illustrated

Military Modelling

BADGES OF THE BRITISH ARMY
1820 to 1987

1. The 17th (Leicestershire) Regiment of Foot. Other ranks' shoulder belt plate, late 18th century. Brass.

2. The 11th (North Devon) Regiment of Foot. Other ranks' shoulder belt plate, 18th century. Brass.

3. The Devizes Association (early 19th-century volunteer unit). Shoulder belt plate, incorporating castle from town's coat of arms. Gilded brass.

4. Officers' helmet plate for the 1812, Waterloo Pattern shako. Gilded. Regiments with special badges had the emblems impressed below a smaller cipher.

5. London and Westminster Light Horse Volunteers. Shoulder belt plate, late 18th century. White metal.

6. The Royal East India Volunteers, 2nd Regiment (London volunteer unit). Shoulder belt plate. Gilded, hallmarked for 1796.

7. The Loyal Chelmsford Volunteers (formed 1803). Shoulder belt plate. Gilded.

8. The 2nd (Queen's Royal) Regiment of Foot. Officers' shoulder belt plate. Silver, hallmarked for 1791.

9

10

12

13

9. The 62nd (The Wiltshire) Regiment of Foot. Other ranks' shoulder belt plate, *circa* 1840. Stamped brass.
10. The 41st (Welch) Regiment of Foot. Officers' shoulder belt plate. The blue enamel centre was introduced in 1831.
11. The 9th (The East Norfolk) Regiment of Foot. Shoulder belt plate. The separate figure of Britannia is pinned to the plate. Brass.
12. The 25th (The King's Own Borderers) Regiment of Foot. Elaborate shoulder belt plate, *circa* 1850. A slider was also worn on the belt.
13. The 9th (The East Norfolk) Regiment of Foot. Other ranks' shoulder belt plate. Pressed brass.
14. The 86th (Royal County Down) Regiment of Foot. Other ranks' shoulder belt plate, *circa* 1850. It was attached to the belt by four broad hooks instead of the more usual two hooks and two lugs. Pressed brass.

15

16

18

19

17

20

15. The Bloomsbury Rifles, raised in 1860; later became a Volunteer Battalion in The Rifle Brigade. Bronze-coloured helmet plate.
16. The Norfolk Regiment. Home Service Pattern helmet plate. Central Britannia and motto in white metal. King's crown dates this to post-1902.
17. The Norfolk Regiment. Other ranks' shako plate with typical double dome of Queen Victoria's crown (QVC); worn 1869–79.
18. The 24th County of London Battalion. Home Service Pattern helmet plate with King's crown; central paschal lamb mounted on red material.
19. The 4th Volunteer Battalion, The Queen's Royal West Surrey Regiment. Belt fitting with QVC and a threaded screw fitting. White metal.
20. The 7th City of London Battalion, The London Regiment. Formed in 1908. Other ranks' Full Dress helmet plate.

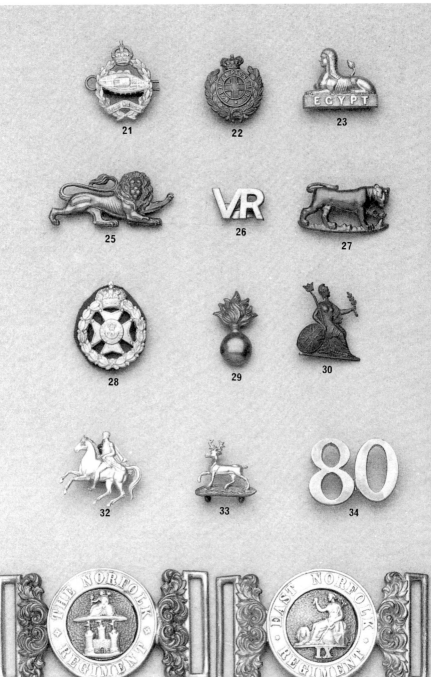

21 22 23

25 26 27

28 29 30

32 33 34

36 37

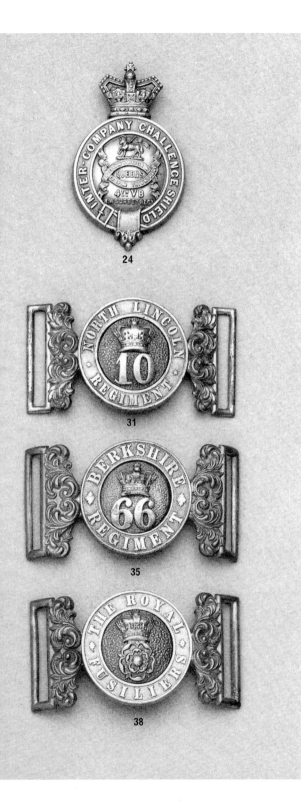

21. The Tank Corps. One of a pair of opposite-facing collar badges or 'dogs'.
22. The Northamptonshire Regiment. Collar badge.
23. The Lincolnshire Regiment. Collar badge.
24. The 4th Volunteer Battalion, The Royal West Surrey Regiment. Shooting badge worn on left sleeve of tunic. White metal.
25. The King's Own (Royal Lancaster Regiment). Collar dog.
26. Royal Air Force Volunteer Reserve. Collar dog. Brass.
27. The Gordon Highlanders. Collar dog.
28. The Bloomsbury Rifles. Collar dog, *circa* 1900. White metal.
29. The 7th City of London Battalion. Flaming grenade collar dog.
30. The Norfolk Regiment. Collar dog.
31. The 10th (North Lincoln) Regiment of Foot. Waist belt clasp, pre-1881. Bimetal.
32. Oxford University Officer's Training Corps (Cavalry). Collar dog. White metal.
33. The Hertfordshire and Bedfordshire Yeomanry. Collar dog. Bimetal.
34. The 80th (Staffordshire Volunteers) Regiment of Foot. Numeral worn on the round, 'pork-pie' Undress cap. Brass.
35. The 66th (Berkshire) Regiment of Foot. Waist belt clasp, pre-1881. Bimetal.
36. The Norfolk Regiment. Waist belt clasp, *circa* 1900. Bimetal.
37. The Norfolk Regiment. Waist belt clasp, pre-1881.
38. The Royal Fusiliers. Victorian waist belt clasp.

39

40

41

42

44

45

46

47

48

49

50

51

53

54

55

43

52

56

39. The Duke of Cornwall's Light Infantry. Other ranks' tunic button, post-1929.

40. Royal Engineers' Department. Officers' button with QVC and cipher. Gilded.

41. Although similar to military buttons, this is an early London Post Office button.

42. Ordnance Store. Officers' button, *circa* 1880. Gilded.

43. The Westminster Volunteers. Belt fitting, 19th century. White metal.

44. General Officers' button, 19th century. Gilded.

45. Oxford University Rifle Volunteers (OURV). Button, mid 19th century. White metal.

46. Medical Staff. Officers' button, *circa* 1880. Gilded.

47. Cinque Port Rifle Volunteers. Button, late 19th century. White metal.

48. The Royal Air Force. Other ranks' button, pre-1953. Brass.

49. RAF. Officers' button of same period.

50. The Air Training Corps. Button. White metal.

51. The Holborn Battalion, The Rifle Volunteers. Lapel badge.

52. The 38th Corps of Rifle Volunteers (formed in 1860). Belt fitting. As this badge uses the title 'Artists' it must postdate 1877 when this distinction was introduced.

53. British Airborne Forces. Shoulder patch, Second World War. Cloth.

54. Lapel brooch for those who rendered special services during the First World War; each is numbered on the back. White metal.

55. London Metropolitan Special Constabulary. Cap badge, pre-1953. White metal.

56. The 28th County of London Battalion (Artists Rifles). Second pattern badge.

57

58

61

63

64

66

67

68

69

70

71

57. The 2nd (Queen's Royal) Regiment of Foot. Shako plate. Bimetal.

58. The Second (Queen's Royal) Regiment of Foot. Shako plate, Brass.

59. Regimental numeral. Brass.

60. Shoulder title. Brass.

61. Badge adopted in 1924. Gilding metal.

62. 4th Volunteer Battalion of the regiment. White metal.

63. Forage cap badge, 1898–1921. Bimetal.

64. 22nd County of London Battalion (The Queen's). 1908–22.

65. Cranleigh School Cadet Force. One of the Officer's Training Corps, known from 1948 as the Combined Cadet Force.

66. Badge worn as a unit of the Territorial Force, 1908–21. Blackened brass.

67. The 3rd Volunteer Battalion, The East Surrey Regiment. With QVC. Bronze.

68. The Queen's Regiment. Badge introduced in 1966. Anodized.

69. Collar dog of this regiment, worn 1908–22.

70. Badge of The Queen's Royal Surrey Regiment, formed when The Queen's Royal Regiment (West Surrey) and The East Surrey Regiment were amalgamated in 1959. Anodized.

71. Another version of the collar dog.

72. The 4th Volunteer Battalion, The East Surrey Regiment. Bronze.

73

74

76

78

79

73. The Royal Fusiliers (City of London Regiment). Other ranks' grenade badge for the busby-like racoon skin head-dress worn by the various Fusilier regiments post-1901. Brass.
74. The Royal Irish Fusiliers (Princess Victoria's). Brass.
75. The Northumberland Fusiliers. Brass.
76. The Royal Welsh Fusiliers. Brass.
77. The Royal Inniskilling Fusiliers. Officers' glengarry badge, post-1881. Brass.
78. The Royal Fusiliers (City of London Regiment). Similar to **73**, but with QVC.
79. The Lancashire Fusiliers. White metal.
80. The Royal Scots Fusiliers (with KC).

81   82   83   84

86   87   88

90   91   92

95

96

81. The Royal Flying Corps. Unusual other ranks' badge with slider. Brass.
82. RFC. The more usual form, with lugs to secure it to cap.
83. RAF. Cap badge with KC. Brass.
84. RAF. Cap badge introduced in 1942. Plastic, secured by two bendable brass strips.
85. The Army Air Corps, 1957. Anodized.
86. RAF. Cap badge with QC, 1953. Brass.
87. The Army Air Corps, worn 1942–50. Unusual in that it is of hallmarked silver.
88. RAF. Physical Training Instructors' sleeve badge. Brass.
89. The Parachute Regiment. Badge worn from 1943 until 1953 when QC was adopted. White metal.
90. RAF. Officers' badge for peaked cap.
91. RAF. Officers' Dress helmet badge. Bimetal.
92. The Glider Pilot Regiment. Badge with slider adopted in 1955. Anodized.
93. The Parachute Regiment. Collar dogs, pre-1953.
94. The Glider Pilot Regiment. Earlier version.
95. Special Air Service Regiment. Brass badge with wire fittings.
96. SAS. Badge worn from 1953. Bimetal.
97. RAF. Sleeve badge worn by Wireless Operators, Radio and Wireless Mechanics. Cloth.

37

98

99

100

102

103

104

107

108

109

112

113

114

98. Leeds Rifles (Cockburn High School Cadets). Brass.

99. The 5th (Cinque Ports) Battalion, The Royal Sussex Regiment. White metal.

100. The 6th City of London Battalion (City of London Rifles). Bronze.

101. The 5th City of London Battalion (Rifle Brigade). White metal.

102. The Rifle Brigade (Prince Consort's Own). Badge worn 1934–57. White metal.

103. The King's Royal Rifle Corps. With KC. Black.

104. The Buckinghamshire Battalion, The Oxfordshire and Buckinghamshire Light Infantry. Black.

105. 3/4th County of London Yeomanry (Sharpshooters). Bimetal.

106. The 23rd County of London Battalion, The London Regiment. Bimetal.

107. The 16th County of London Battalion (Queen's Westminster Rifles). Worn 1908–22. Black.

108. The Queen's Royal Rifles. Worn 1961. Brass.

109. The 9th County of London Battalion (Queen Victoria's). Brass.

110. The 3rd County of London (Sharp Shooters) Imperial Yeomanry.

111. The 7th City of London Battalion. Bimetal.

112. The 11th County of London Battalion (Finsbury Rifles). Brass.

113. The 12th County of London Battalion (The Rangers). Black.

114. The King's Royal Rifle Corps Cadets. The motto *Celer et Audax* beneath the crown replaced by *Fight the Good Fight* and *CLB Cadets*.

115. The 21st County of London Battalion (First Surrey Rifles). Black.

116. The 3rd County of London Yeomanry (The Sharpshooters) (Hussars).

117

118

120

121

123

125

126

117. The Cameronians (Scottish Rifles). Piper's badge, 1921–68. White metal.
118. The Northumberland Fusiliers: 20th, 21st, 22nd and 29th Battalions (Tyneside Scottish), 1914–18. White metal.
119. The Scottish Horse. A composite badge, possibly for a slouch hat.
120. The Cameronians (Scottish Rifles). White metal.
121. The Lowland Brigade. Worn 1959–68. Anodized.
122. Lovat's Scouts. Worn 1903–20. White metal.
123. The 9th (Glasgow Highlanders) Battalion, The Highland Light Infantry (City of Glasgow Regiment). Post-1953. White metal.
124. The 10th (Scottish) Battalion, The King's (Liverpool) Regiment. Worn 1908–37. White metal.
125. The Highland Regiment. Other ranks' badge worn from 1942 until disbanded in 1949. White metal.
126. The Lowland Regiment. Similar dates. White metal.
127. The Seaforth Highlanders (Ross-shire Buffs, The Duke of Albany's). Badge worn 1898–1921. White metal.

128

129

133

134

135

137

138

128. The Militia Artillery. Helmet plate worn from 1891 when the title Militia Artillery replaced Artillery Militia. White metal.

129. The Territorial Force. Artillery helmet plate. Laurel spray above gun replaces motto *Ubique* found on plates of the regular units.

130. The Honourable Artillery Company. Officers' forage cap badge, post-1902. Gilded.

131. The Honourable Artillery Company. Worn by Warrant Officers and sergeants. Initials in white metal.

132. The Honourable Artillery Company. Other ranks' cap badge. Brass.

133. The Royal Horse Artillery. Collar dog with KC, 1936–53.

134/5. The Royal Horse Artillery. A pair of collar dogs with QC, 1953.

136. Royal Artillery. Cap badge with KC. Brass.

137. A Cadet Company. Helmet plate with QVC so pre-1901.

138. Cinque Ports Artillery Volunteers. Helmet plate with QVC.

139. Royal Malta Artillery. With KC.

140. Royal Artillery. Badge with KC. Wheel on gun mounted separately.

141

143

145

142

144

146

141. The Royal Marine Light Infantry. Helmet plate worn from 1905. Brass.
142. The Royal East Middlesex Militia. Glengarry badge, 1874–81. White metal.
143. The Royal Malta Militia. Shako plate with KC. Bimetal.
144. The 11th (Royal Militia Island of Jersey) Battalion, The Hampshire Regiment. This unit was only in being from 1940 until 1946.
145. The Middlesex Regiment. Helmet plate with KC (lacking top cross). Bimetal.
146. The Royal Malta Militia. Bimetal.

147

148

149

151

152

153

155

156

157

159

160

161

150

154

158

162

163

147. The Royal Engineers. Forage cap badge with cipher of King George V. The centre was left unvoided as an economy measure during the First World War.

148. Similar badge, with cipher of King George VI and voided centre.

149. Similar badge with cipher of white metal.

150. The Machine Gun Corps. Cap badge, 1915–22.

151. The Royal Army Medical Corps. Cap badge with KC. Brass.

152. RAMC. Badge with St Edward's crown, adopted 1953. Bimetal.

153. The Army Service Corps. Badge worn from 1916 until 1918 when the prefix Royal was added. Brass.

154. The Machine Gun Corps. Officers' collar dog. Bronze.

155. RAMC. Badge with St. Edward's crown, adopted in 1953. Brass.

156. Royal Army Service Corps. Badge with King George VI cipher and voided centre.

157. The Royal Corps of Transport, formed in 1965. Anodized.

158. Crossed axes worn by pioneers in the Infantry, and in some units combined with grenade (Guards), a star (Scots and Irish Guards) and a bugle (light infantry or rifle regiments). Brass.

159. The School of Musketry. Badge worn 1902–19.

160. The Army Physical Training Staff. Forage cap badge worn from 1902.

161. Smaller version of same badge.

162. What appears to be a British collar dog is in fact Belgian. Take care!

163. Artificers' badge worn by armourer sergeants, machinery artificers and smiths.

164

165

166

168

169

170

172

173

174

176

177

178

167

171

175

179

164. The 1/1st London Divisional Cyclist Company, formed in 1916. Voided badge. Brass.

165. The Army Cyclist Corps, formed in 1914. The wheel has 16 spokes; another version has 12. Brass.

166. The 25th County of London (Cyclist) Battalion. Brass.

167. The 15th County of London Battalion (Prince of Wales's Own Civil Service Rifles). Badge worn from 1908. Brass.

168. Inns of Court OTC, incorporating the badges of the various Inns or legal centres of London. Brass.

169. The 5th City of London Battalion (London Rifle Brigade), Cadets. Post-1908. Brass.

170. The Westminster (Yeomanry) Dragoons. Badge worn 1908–22. White metal.

171. The 13th County of London Battalion (Kensington).

172. The Paddington Rifles, 1908–12 when it was replaced by The 10th County of London Regiment (Hackney).

173. The 19th County of London Battalion (St Pancras). Brass.

174. The 20th County of London Battalion (Blackheath and Woolwich). Bimetal.

175. The 18th County of London Battalion (London Irish Rifles). White metal.

176. City of London Imperial Yeomanry (Rough Riders). Bimetal.

177. The 14th County of London Battalion (London Scottish). Worn 1908. White metal.

178. The 10th County of London Battalion (Hackney), post-1912. This unit replaced The Paddington Rifles (see 172). Brass.

179. The 28th County of London Battalion (Artists' Rifles). White metal.

180

181

184

185

186

187

190

191

192

194

195

196

197

198

180. The Life Guards. Centre voided with cipher of King George VI. This unit was formed in 1922 when the 1st and 2nd Life Guards were amalgamated.

181. The 2nd Life Guards, with cipher of King George V, first issued in 1914. Brass.

182. The Scots Guards. Brass.

183. The Scots Guards. Badge worn by sergeants and musicians. White metal.

184. The Life Guards, with cipher of Queen Elizabeth II, post-1953.

185. The 1st Life Guards.

186. The Royal Horse Guards (The Blues), post-1953.

187. The Blues and Royals. Regiment formed in 1969 by amalgamation of The Royal Horse Guards (The Blues) and The Royal Dragoons (1st Dragoons). Brass.

188. Irish Guards. Brass.

189. The Coldstream Guards. Other ranks', 1905–. Brass.

190. The Household Cavalry. Cipher of Queen Elizabeth II.

191. The Grenadier Guards. Flaming grenade; plain for other ranks.

192. The Grenadier Guards. Similar, but with lugs in place of the slider.

193. The Scots Guards. Badge with lugs for attachment to belt or pouch. White metal.

194. The Grenadier Guards. With impressed GR cipher mirrored. Worn by sergeants.

195. The Grenadier Guards. Royal cipher applied and not impressed. Worn by sergeants and commissioned quartermasters. White metal.

196. The Welsh Guards. Shoulder title. White metal.

197. The Welsh Guards. Cap badge worn from 1915 when the regiment was formed. Brass.

198. The Welsh Guards. Badge worn on the puggaree. Brass.

199. The Grenadier Guards. This badge was also worn on the puggaree or, as shown, with the initials GG as a shoulder title. Brass.

200

201

203

206

207

204

208

209

210

211

213

214

216

217

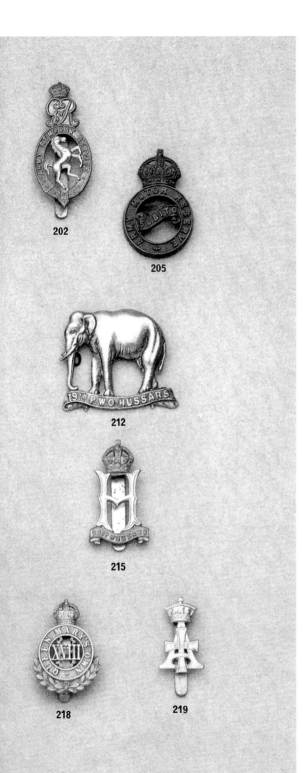

200. The Royal Armoured Corps. Plastic, 1943.
201. The Royal Armoured Corps. White metal, from 1953.
202. Army Remount Service. Bimetal.
203. The 18th (Victoria Mary, Princess of Wales's Own) Hussars. Other ranks', 1905–10. The title was changed in 1911, and the regiment was amalgamated with The 13th Hussars in 1922.
204. The Reconnaissance Corps. White metal, 1942–6.
205. Army Motor Reserve. Brass.
206. The 21st (Empress of India's) Lancers, 1901–22.
207. The 25th Dragoons, 1941–8.
208. The Tank Corps, formed in 1917. Brass.
209. The Royal Tank Corps. White metal badge introduced in 1922 when corps received prefix 'Royal' and motto *Fear Naught*. There are two versions with tanks facing opposite directions.
210. Post-1953 version of badge.
211. The Royal Armoured Corps, 1939–41.
212. The 19th (Queen Alexandra's Own Royal) Hussars. White metal, 1898–1902.
213. The Tank Corps. Sleeve badge. Brass.
214. The Tank Corps. Officers' version. Bronze.
215. The 23rd Hussars. Bimetal, 1941–8.
216. The Royal Tank Regiment. Shoulder tab. Cloth.
217. The Royal Tank Regiment. Shoulder title. Brass.
218. The 18th (Queen Mary's Own) Royal Hussars. 1910–19.
219. The 19th (Queen Alexandra's Own Royal) Hussars. 1909–22 (see 212).

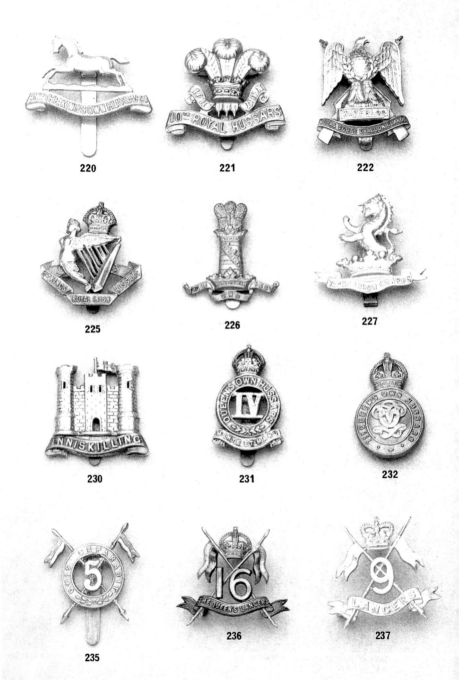

220

221

222

225

226

227

230

231

232

235

236

237

220. The 3rd (King's Own) Hussars. Bimetal, 1920–58.
221. The 10th Royal Hussars. Bimetal, 1896–1969.
222. The Royal Scots Dragoon Guards. Bimetal, 1971.
223. The 14th (King's) Hussars. Until 1915.
224. The 6th Dragoon Guards (Carabineers). Bimetal, 1902–22.
225. The 8th (King's Royal Irish) Hussars. Bimetal, 1904–54.
226. The 11th (Prince Albert's Own) Hussars. Until 1969.
227. The 7th (The Princess Royal's) Dragoon Guards. 1898–1906.
228. The 15th (The King's) Hussars. Bimetal, 1902–22.
229. The 1st (Royal) Dragoons. 1902–22.
230. The 6th (Inniskilling) Dragoons. Bimetal, until 1922.
231. The 4th (Queen's Own) Hussars. 1907–54.
232. The 7th (Queen's Own) Hussars. 1901–55.
233. The 5th (Princess Charlotte of Wales's) Dragoon Guards. Bimetal, 1902–22.
234. The 13th Hussars. Bimetal, 1902–22.
235. The 5th (Royal Irish) Lancers. Bimetal, 1896–22.
236. The 16th (The Queen's) Lancers. Bimetal, 1905–22.
237. The 9th Queen's Royal Lancers. Anodized, 1954–60.
238. The 12th Royal Lancers (Prince of Wales's). Bimetal, 1930–54.
239. The Royal Dragoons (1st Dragoons). Bimetal, 1949–69.

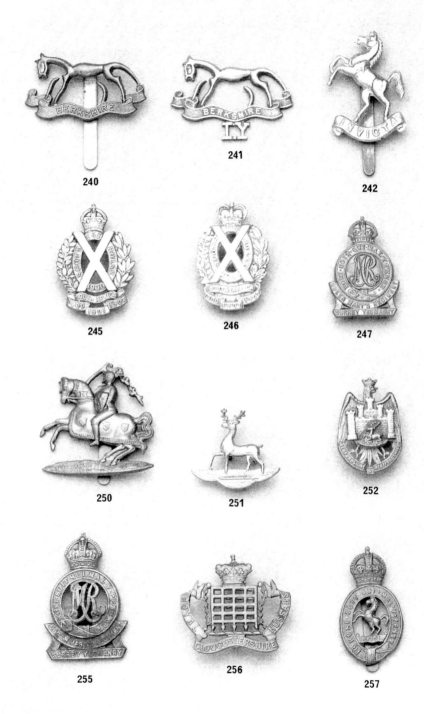

240

241

242

245

246

247

250

251

252

255

256

257

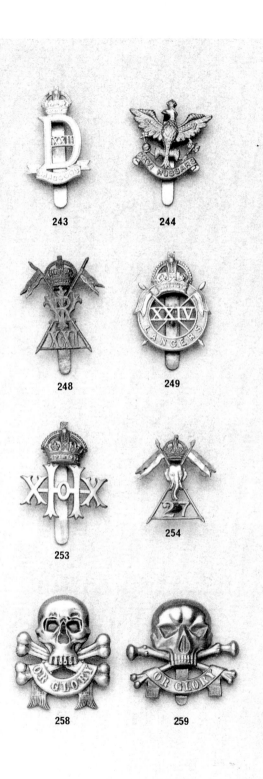

243

244

248

249

253

254

258

259

240. The Royal Berkshire (Hungerford) Yeomanry (Dragoons). Brass, 1908–22.
241. Berkshire Imperial Yeomanry. White metal, 1901–08.
242. The Queen's Own West Kent Yeomanry (Hussars). 1908–22.
243. The 22nd Dragoons. White metal, 1940–8.
244. The 26th Hussars. Brass, 1940–8.
245. The Scottish Horse. Raised in 1900 for the Imperial Yeomanry. Brass.
246. Similar badge with Scottish crown. White metal.
247. The Queen Mary's Surrey Yeomanry (Lancers). 1910–22. White metal.
248. The 21st (Empress of India's) Lancers. Economy brass issue from 1916.
249. The 24th Lancers. White metal, 1940–8.
250. The Fife and Forfarshire Yeomanry (Dragoons). Found in brass and white metal, 1908–22.
251. The Hertfordshire Yeomanry (Dragoons). Brass, 1908–22.
252. The Bedfordshire and Hertfordshire Regiment. Bimetal, 1919–58.
253. The 20th Hussars. 1908–22. Brass.
254. The 27th Lancers. Bimetal, 1940–8.
255. The Queen Mary's Surrey Yeomanry (Lancers). With voided centre (see 247).
256. The Royal Gloucestershire Hussars (a unit of the Imperial Yeomanry). 1902–8.
257. The Duke of Connaught's Own Royal East Kent Yeomanry (Mounted Rifles). 1908–22.
258. The 17th (Duke of Cambridge's Own) Lancers. NCOs' arm badge. White metal.
259. Similar badge in brass. In 1922 the regiment was amalgamated with The 21st (Empress of India's) Lancers to form The 17th/21st Lancers.

263

268

272

277

260. The Royal Irish Rifles. White metal, 1913–52. The title was changed to The Royal Ulster Rifles in 1920.
261. The Royal Irish Rangers. Anodized, 1968.
262. The North Irish Horse. Brass, 1908–52.
263. The Dublin County Light Infantry. Glengarry badge, post-1881. White metal.
264. The Connaught Rangers. Officers' badge, 1902–22. Bronze.
265. The 8th Irish Battalion, The King's (Liverpool Regiment). Brass, 1908–21.
266. The Connaught Rangers. Brass, 1902–22.
267. The Northumberland Fusiliers: 24th–27th and 30th Battalions (Tyneside Irish), 1914–18. Brass.
268. The Dublin Regiment National Volunteers. Brass.
269. The Royal Dublin Fusiliers. Officers' badge, 1881–1922. Bronze.
270. The North of Ireland Imperial Yeomanry. Collar dog, 1901–8. White metal.
271. The Royal Dublin Fusiliers. Bimetal, 1881–1922.
272. The 14th Battalion (Young Citizens), The Royal Irish Rifles. Brass, 1914–18.
273. The Royal Ulster Rifles. White metal, 1920. Doubtful if original badge.
274. The Royal Munster Fusiliers. Bimetal, 1898–1921.
275. The Prince of Wales's Leinster Regiment (Royal Canadians). Bimetal, 1881–1922.
276. The Royal Inniskilling Fusiliers. Bimetal, 1881–1958; except during the late 1920s and early 1930s when the grenade was discarded.
277. The South Irish Horse. Brass, 1908–22.

278

279

282

283

285

286

288

289

278. The King's Own Scottish Borderers. White metal, 1887–1902.

279. The King's Own Scottish Borderers. White metal, post–1902.

280. The Highland Light Infantry. With small scroll, white metal, 1902–52.

281. The Highland Light Infantry. With large scroll, white metal, 1902–52.

282. The Queen's Own Cameron Highlanders. White metal, 1898–1961.

283. The Queen's Own Cameron Highlanders. Badge for feather bonnet and glengarry. White metal.

284. The Queen's Own Cameron Highlanders (The Liverpool Scottish). White metal, post-1938.

285. The Argyll and Sutherland Highlanders (Princess Louise's). Officers' collar dog. Bronze.

286. The Argyll and Sutherland Highlanders (Princess Louise's). Other ranks' collar dog. White metal.

287. The Royal Scots (Royal Regiment). Bimetal with red (1st Battalion) or green (2nd Battalion) cloth backing at centre, 1920–58, and from 1969.

288. The Princess Louise's (Argyll and Sutherland Highlanders). White metal with solid centre, 1882–1900.

289. Similar, but with voided centre.

290. The Highland Brigade. Anodized, 1959–68.

291

292

293

296

297

298

300

301

304

305

306

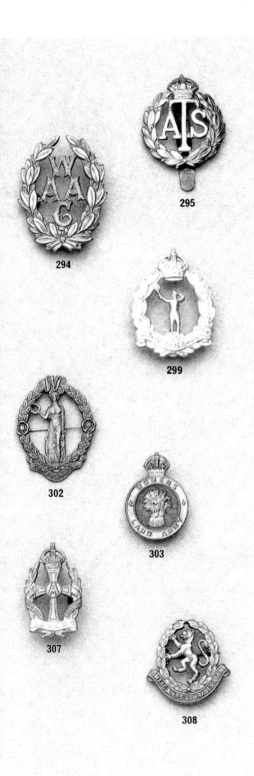

291. Oxford University OTC (Infantry). White metal.
292. The King's (Shropshire Light Infantry). Bimetal.
293. The Duke of Cornwall's Light Infantry. White metal.
294. The Women's Army Auxiliary Corps, formed in 1917. Brass.
295. Auxiliary Territorial Service (women's service formed in 1938). Brass.
296. Prince Albert's (Somerset Light Infantry). White metal.
297. Prince Albert's (Somerset Light Infantry): 4th and 5th Battalions.
298. The Durham Light Infantry. White metal, 1902–53.
299. The Royal Observer Corps.
300. The York and Lancaster Regiment. Bimetal, 1881–1969.
301. The Cambridgeshire Regiment. Formed in 1908. Bimetal. The title is also found spelt as Cambridgshire.
302. The Women's Legion. Formed in 1915 and absorbed into the WAAC in 1917. White metal.
303. The Women's Land Army. Reformed in 1939. With green enamel centre.
304. The King's Own Yorkshire Light Infantry. Bimetal, 1898–1958.
305. The Loyal North Lancashire Regiment. Bimetal, 1901–20.
306. The Loyal (North Lancashire) Regiment. Bimetal, 1921–53.
307. Queen Alexandra's Royal Army Nursing Corps. 1949–53.
308. Queen Mary's Army Auxiliary Corps and Army Territorial Service, Old Comrades' Association.

309

310

311

313

314

315

317

318

319

321

322

323

312

316

320

324

309. The Sherwood Foresters (The Derbyshire Regiment). Bimetal, 1898–1901.
310. The Sherwood Foresters (The Derbyshire Regiment). Belt or pouch fitting. Bimetal.
311. The 4th Battalion, Duke of Edinburgh's (The Wiltshire Regiment). Black, 1916–47.
312. The Border Regiment. White metal, 1901–53.
313. The Sherwood Foresters (Nottinghamshire and Derbyshire Regiment). Officers' badge, 1902–53. Bronze.
314. The Essex Volunteer Regiment. Brass, 1914–18.
315. The East Anglian Brigade. Formed in 1957/8 and changed to The Royal Anglian Regiment in 1968. White metal.
316. The 5th Battalion, The Border Regiment. White metal, with South Africa battle honour.
317. The Northamptonshire Regiment. With castle and flag. Brass, 1898–1921.
318. The Northamptonshire Regiment. Without flag and key. Bimetal.
319. The Essex Regiment. Bronze, 1908–58.
320. The Prince of Wales's Volunteers (The South Lancashire Regiment). Bimetal, 1920–58.
321. The Duke of Cambridge's Own (Middlesex Regiment). Bimetal, 1898–1921.
322. The same badge, but plastic, *circa* 1943.
323. The East Yorkshire Regiment. Bimetal, 1898–1958.
324. The 2nd King Edward's Horse. Brass, 1914–24.

325

326

327

330

331

332

335

336

337

339

340

341

325. The Duke of Lancaster's Own Yeomanry (Dragoons). Brass, 1908–51.
326. The South Nottinghamshire (Yeomanry) Hussars. Brass, 1908–52.
327. Westmoreland and Cumberland Yeomanry. Brass, 1908–22.
328. The Lincolnshire Yeomanry (Lancers). Brass, 1908–22.
329. The Prince Albert's Own Leicestershire Yeomanry (Hussars). Brass, 1922–56.
330. The Essex Yeomanry. Brass, 1916–54.
331. The Imperial Yeomanry. General Service badge worn on the slouch hat, 1901–8. Brass, with red and blue rosette.
332. The Duke of Lancaster's Own Yeomanry (Dragoons). Bimetal.
333. The Shropshire Yeomanry. Brass, 1908–50.
334. The Earl of Chester's Cheshire Yeomanry (Hussars). Brass, 1908–22.
335. The Queen's Own (Royal West Kent) Regiment. White metal, 1898–1958.
336. The Queen's Own Yorkshire Yeomanry (Dragoons). White metal, 1951–6.
337. The 1st Battalion, The Monmouthshire Regiment. White metal, 1908–25.
338. The Queen's Own Worcestershire (Yeomanry) Hussars. Bimetal, 1908–56.
339. The Brecknockshire Battalion, The South Wales Borderers. Brass, 1908–22.
340. The Duke of York's Own Loyal Suffolk (Yeomanry) Hussars. Bimetal, 1908–61.
341. The Glamorganshire Yeomanry (Dragoons). Bimetal, 1908–22.
342. The Derbyshire Yeomanry (Dragoons). Brass, 1908–57.

343

344

345

348

349

350

354

353

355

358

359

360

343. The Dorsetshire Regiment. Bimetal, 1898–1901.
344. The Dorsetshire Regiment. Bimetal, 1901–56.
345. The Royal Warwickshire Regiment. Bimetal, 1898–1958.
346. The Hampshire Yeomanry (Carabineers). Brass, 1916–51.
347. The Northumberland (Yeomanry) Hussars. Brass, 1908–56.
348. The Duke of Wellington's (West Riding Regiment). Officers' collar dog. Bronze.
349. The Prince of Wales's Own (West Yorkshire Regiment). Bimetal, 1898–1958.
350. The Duke of Wellington's (West Riding Regiment). Bimetal, 1897–1970.
351. The Alexandra, Princess of Wales's Own Yorkshire Yeomanry (Hussars). Bimetal, 1908–56.
352. The 2nd Northamptonshire Yeomanry. White metal, 1939–45.
353. Alexandra, Princess of Wales's Own (Yorkshire Regiment). Brass, 1898–1908.
354. The East Lancashire Regiment. Officers' collar dog. Bronze.
355. The East Lancashire Regiment. Bimetal, 1930–54.
356. The Welsh (Yeomanry) Horse (Lancers). Brass, 1914–21.
357. The Pembrokeshire (Castlemain) Yeomanry (Hussars). Bimetal, 1908–71.
358. The Green Howards (Alexandra, Princess of Wales's Own Yorkshire Regiment). Bronze, 1903–50.
359. The King's Regiment (Liverpool). Bimetal, 1927–50.
360. The Green Howards (Alexandra, Princess of Wales's Own Yorkshire Regiment). Badge worn 1950–8, and 1969–. Anodized.
361. The Royal Buckinghamshire (Yeomanry) Hussars. Brass, 1908–52.
362. The Huntingdonshire Cyclist Battalion. Brass, 1914–18. Also The Huntingdonshire Home Guard, 1951–7.

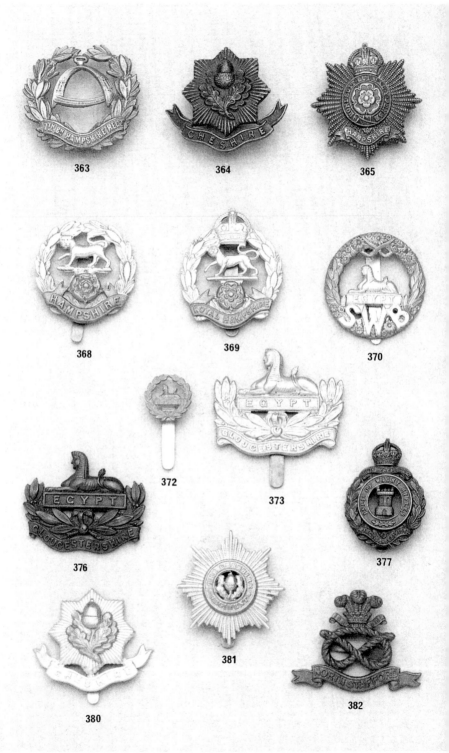

363

364

365

368

369

370

372

373

376

377

381

380

382

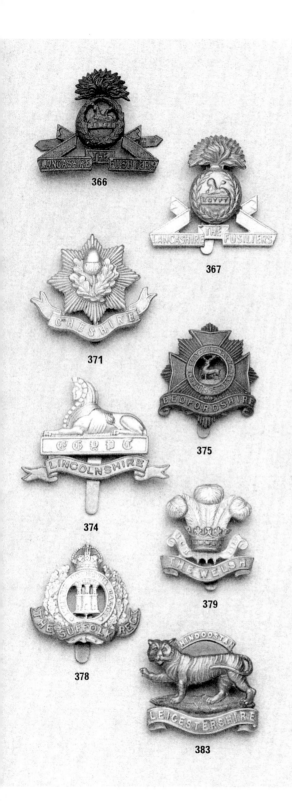

363. The 7th Battalion, The Hampshire Regiment. Brass, 1908–21.

364. The Cheshire Regiment. Bronze, 1898–1921.

365. The Hampshire Regiment. Officers' pattern. Bimetal.

366. The Lancashire Fusiliers. Officers' badge, 1898–1921. Bronze.

367. The Lancashire Fusiliers. Bimetal, 1898–1921.

368. The Hampshire Regiment. Bimetal, 1898–1921.

369. The Royal Hampshire Regiment. Bimetal, 1947–53.

370. The South Wales Borderers. Bimetal, 1898–1969.

371. The Cheshire Regiment. Bimetal, 1898–1921.

372. The Gloucestershire Regiment. Brass badge worn on rear of head-dress.

373. The Gloucestershire Regiment. White metal, 1898–1958.

374. The Lincolnshire Regiment. Bimetal, 1898–1947.

375. The Bedfordshire Regiment. Brass, 1898–1919.

376. The 4th Battalion, The Gloucestershire Regiment. Blackened brass, 1898–1958.

377. The 8th (Isle of Wight Rifles, Princess Beatrice's) Battalion, The Hampshire Regiment. Black, 1908–21.

378. The Suffolk Regiment. Bimetal, 1901–55.

379. The Welsh Regiment. Bimetal, 1898 until 1920 when it became Welch.

380. The Cheshire Regiment. Bimetal, 1898–1921. See **370** with larger scroll.

381. The Cheshire Regiment. Bimetal, 1922–58 and post-1969.

382. The Prince of Wales's (North Staffordshire Regiment). Bronze, 1898–1959.

383. The Leicestershire Regiment. Bimetal, 1898–1951.

384

385

386

388

389

390

392

393

394

395

397

398

384. The Army Educational Corps. Brass, 1927–46.
385. Yeomanry Cadets. KC. Brass.
386. Army Apprentices' School. Piper's badge. White metal, 1954.
387. The Royal Naval Mine Watching Service.
388. The Royal Military Academy, Woolwich. Gilded, gilt and bronze, 1902–47.
389. The Royal Military College, Sandhurst. White metal, 1947–53.
390. The Royal Army Pay Corps. Bimetal, 1929–53.
391. Drake Battalion, The Royal Naval Division. Bimetal, 1916–18.
392. The Royal Army Educational Corps. Bimetal, 1946–54.
393. The Royal Army Educational Corps. Bimetal, 1954–.
394. The Mobile Defence Corps. Bimetal, 1955–9.
395. The Royal Army Pay Corps. Brass, 1920–29.
396. Anson Battalion, The Royal Naval Division. Brass, 1916–18.
397. The Army Catering Corps. Bimetal, 1941–54.
398. The Army Catering Corps. Brass, 1941–54.
399. Royal Navy. Officers' cap badge.

400

401

402

404

405

406

409

410

411

414

415

416

400. The Manchester Regiment. Bimetal, 1898–1923.
401. The Manchester Regiment. Brass, 1923–58. Also in white metal.
402. The Manchester Regiment. Bimetal, 1898–1923. With different style of lettering.
403. The East Anglian Brigade. Anodized, 1958.
404. The Royal Norfolk Regiment. Brass, 1937–58.
405. The Norfolk Regiment. Bimetal, 1898–1937.
406. The Norfolk Regiment. Bronze.
407. The Devonshire Regiment. Bimetal, 1903–55.
408. The Devonshire Regiment. Blackened brass, 1920–47.
409. The Herefordshire Regiment. Bimetal, 1908–47.
410. The Buffs (East Kent Regiment). Brass, 1896–1961.
411. The Herefordshire Regiment. Officers' badge. Bronze.
412. The Royal Northumberland Fusiliers. Bimetal, 1935–59.
413. The Worcestershire Regiment. Bimetal, 1925–66.
414. The Suffolk Regiment. Brass, 1901–52.
415. The Worcestershire Regiment. Brass, 1898–1925.
416. The Suffolk Regiment. White metal.
417. The Northumberland Fusiliers. Brass, pre-1935.

418

419

420

423

424

425

428

429

430

432

433

434

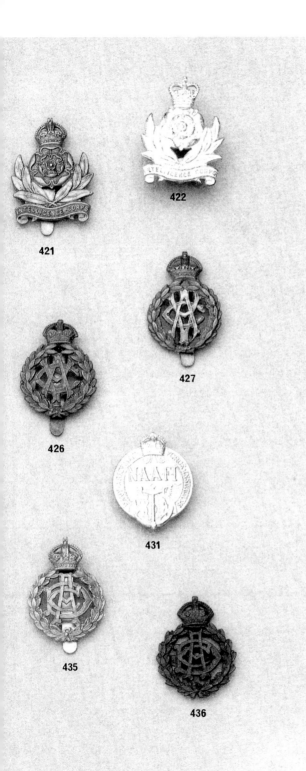

418. The Royal Corps of Signals. Bimetal, 1920–47.
419. The Royal Corps of Signals. Officers' badge. Bronze.
420. Army Ordnance Corps. Brass, 1896–1918.
421. The Intelligence Corps. Brass, 1940–55.
422. The Intelligence Corps. Anodized, 1955.
423. The Royal Army Ordnance Corps. Brass, 1918–47.
424. The Royal Army Ordnance Corps. 1947–49.
425. Oxford University OTC (Signals).
426. Army Veterinary Corps. Brass, 1916.
427. Army Veterinary Corps. Bimetal, 1903–18.
428. The Corps of Royal Military Police. Brass, 1948–53.
429. The Corps of Royal Military Police. Bimetal, 1953.
430. The Military Provost Staff Corps. Brass, 1936–53.
431. Navy, Army and Air Force Institutes (NAAFI). Silver plated.
432. Royal Army Chaplains' Department. Collar dog, 1939–53. Bronze.
433. Army Scripture Readers. Bimetal.
434. Royal Army Dental Corps. Bimetal, 1948–54.
435. Royal Army Dental Corps. Brass, 1921–48.
436. Royal Army Dental Corps. Officers' badge. Bronze.

INDEX TO THE PLATES

Some unit titles have been slightly modified in order to simplify the listing and location of entries, but the relevant captions give the full titles.